The Management Guide to Delegating

Kate Keenan

RR

RAVETTE PUBLISHING

Published by Ravette Publishing
P.O. Box 296
Horsham
West Sussex RH13 8FH
Telephone: (01 403) 711443
Fax: (01 403) 711554

Series Editor – Anne Tauté
Editor – Catriona Scott

Cover design – Jim Wire
Printing & Binding – Cox & Wyman Ltd.
Production – Oval Projects Ltd.

An Oval Project
produced for Ravette Publishing.

Cover – Delegating is a bit like building
a house of cards. If you do not provide a
firm foundation, it will all fall down.

Acknowledgments:
Jeremy Bethell

Contents

This book is dedicated to
those who would like to manage better
but are too busy to begin.

Delegating

Many people agree that delegating is an essential managing activity, but few find it easy to put into practice. They know it is not just a matter of handing over a job and magically it is achieved, and they have misgivings about trusting other people to do their work as they would do it.

But once you know the procedure, you will find it a powerful and productive way of getting tasks completed and releasing you to do more. It not only offers you a chance to offload some of your burden, it also provides an opportunity to develop and cement good relationships with those who are doing the work.

This book examines the issues involved when delegating, and gives practical suggestions about how to get a lot more of your work done overall, by getting some of it done by others.

1. The Need for Delegating

Delegating is an essential activity when managing because there are many times when it is impossible to do everything yourself. If you want your business or organization to function properly, at some stage you will need to delegate a part of your work.

This means handing over some of your authority and control to someone else and making sure that all goes well. Often the mere contemplation of these things is enough to cause you to quail at the prospect and therefore fail to delegate.

Not Being Willing to Delegate

Most people admit that delegating tasks is a good thing to do, but when it actually comes to the point, they tend to find all sorts of excuses why they cannot do so. The sorts of things they are likely to say are:

- "I'm the only one who can do this job."

- "In the time I need to tell someone what to do, I could have done it myself."

- "I'll only end up having to spend time doing it all over again."

- "Nothing that I do can be delegated."

The reluctance you may have about giving away any task that is under your control means that others never get a chance to prove they can do it. It may well be that you are the best person to do the job, but doing it prevents you from doing more.

The belief that it is quicker to do the job yourself than to teach others is a view which guarantees that you end up doing it all yourself. It may well be that time is lost in coaching people, but this is a far better use of your time than continuously getting involved in activities which detract from your efficiency.

Many of the reasons given for not delegating have to do with a perceived lack of time, yet it is a known fact that if time is considered to be the problem, it is usually the will to delegate that is really lacking.

Not Being Organized

It is easy to put off delegating because you have a great deal to do, and have been doing everything for so long, that you cannot begin to sort out which tasks could or should be delegated. This is often due to the fact that:

● Your own level of personal organization is less than ideal, so you deal with work as it turns up, rather than plan what needs to be done.

- You are not able to isolate a specific task to delegate.

- You have not recognized that your own disorganization is at the heart of your inability to delegate.

When things are disorganized, delegating is difficult, if not impossible, to put into practice. Without taking stock of what you are doing you will never know what tasks can and ought to be delegated, nor will you able to explain them to anyone else.

Feeling Irreplaceable

Being reluctant to delegate often stems from a belief that you are irreplaceable and thus the only one who can do a particular job. But if you look at yourself in this way you will be obstructing your own progress. In reality, you need not get involved with day-to-day details, and more tasks can be delegated than you think.

Some things, such as design skills, may be obvious candidates for delegation. Others, such as compiling figures, may be taking up valuable time. So a sensible way of coping is to bring in professional assistance. By assigning both responsibility and a certain amount of authority to outside agencies you can delegate in order to obtain the services you require.

Even if you say there is nobody available to whom

you can delegate ("I can't delegate because I work for myself", or "I can't delegate because there is no-one capable of doing what I need"), think carefully about the way you work. You probably have a number of responsibilities, all of which involve different sets of activities. You may be surprised to realize that it is perfectly possible to delegate something to yourself. To do so, you simply assign yourself specific tasks to do at specific times. For example, if you need to reply to a letter, you do not interrupt some major creative activity to do this, rather you put it on your list to do when you are in an 'administrative mode'.

Not Trusting People

It is discomforting to think that it is not possible to believe others can be trusted but there are several reasons why this may be true:

- You have been let down in the past.

- You do not think that others will be as meticulous or as careful as you would be.

- You fear that others will not be as committed as you are.

Having confidence in others and trusting them to get on with the job may not always come easily since it involves giving up a certain amount of control and allowing people to do things in their own way. If confidence is lacking, the inclination will be to interfere in what they are doing. This is the last thing you should be doing since the key to building up trust is not meddling in a task you have delegated.

Not Accepting Differences

Many people look for someone to carry out a task in exactly the same way as they would. Subconsciously they are looking for a clone of themselves which they can call upon at a moment's notice when an extra pair of hands is wanted. But since this is not yet a viable option, others can only serve to do what is required.

Recognizing other people's strengths and making the most of them is essential. How they carry out the task is of much less importance, provided they achieve what is required.

When assessing the results, you have to take into account the concept of 'good enough'. This means accepting what has been done so long as it is completed to the standard you have specified, even if it has not been done in exactly the same way as you would have done it. So long as the results are 'good enough' and are wholly acceptable, you should be well pleased with them.

Giving Too Much Away

There are those who think they are really good at delegating because they give so many tasks away. But they may not have grasped that there is a considerable difference between delegation and abdication.

If you give too much away it means that:

- People may have responsibility but no authority, so they have little influence in getting things done should others prove uncooperative.

- People can be asked to carry out tasks which are outside their skills and abilities, so they are unlikely to be able to complete them satisfactorily.

- People may not understand how their given task fits into the overall picture, so they are unable to produce their best work for the circumstances.

The consequence is that when people do not achieve results they may become unresponsive and unwilling to take on anything extra. So, despite your attempts to delegate, you end up having to do it all yourself. Even if people do achieve results, they can end up feeling disillusioned because they are doing all the donkey work, while you appear to be taking any credit that is going.

Giving too much away is, in fact, just as bad as not giving away anything at all.

Summary: Getting Going

There are many good reasons for delegating including making better use of your time, developing the skills of others, and being able to get on with other important tasks.

The main barrier that stops people from doing so is that they are reluctant to delegate for fear that they will not get the results they want.

The key to effective delegating is to be able to answer three basic questions:

- What job can I give away?

- What does the job involve?

- What do I need to do to ensure that people know what they are doing?

This is basically what delegating is all about and it is not nearly as exacting as people make out. So all you need to do is get going.

Questions to Ask Yourself

Think about delegating and answer the following questions:

♠ Am I reluctant to delegate because I dread losing control?

♠ Do I avoid delegating because I think it is going to take up too much time?

♠ Do I believe that I am the only one who can do the job?

♠ Do I find it difficult to single out a task to delegate?

♠ Do I find it difficult to trust other people to do a job properly?

♠ Do I have too much to do?

If you have answered 'Yes' to some or all of these questions, you may need to assess your attitude to delegating.

You Will Be Doing Better If...

★ You are willing to concede that delegating could allow you to do more.

★ You realize that it is not productive to do everything yourself.

★ You recognize that you are not the only one who can do a job properly.

★ You are aware that your own disorganization could be preventing you from delegating.

★ You are prepared to trust others to do some of your work.

★ You acknowledge that delegating is a vital part of managing effectively.

2.   Deciding What to Delegate

Deciding to delegate is usually provoked by an acute awareness that you have far too much to do to give each thing the attention it deserves, or that you will not be able to take anything else unless you hand over some of your responsibilities to someone else. Whatever the reason that spurs you into action, when you delegate you need to follow a logical system.

Choosing the Task

It is a great mistake to think that you can delegate any task that takes your fancy, possibly because you do not feel like doing it or because you have to keep someone busy.

Deciding what to delegate requires you to think about everything you do and make a list of the tasks you do under four headings:

● Tasks you **must** delegate. These are jobs which you really should not be doing at all. Very often they are jobs you have always done or jobs which you particularly enjoy and are reluctant to give away to anybody else. Delegating these tasks enables you to make better use of your time while minimizing the risk involved in handing them over to others.

- Tasks you **should** delegate. These are routine jobs which you may never have considered delegating but which other people are quite capable of carrying out. Not only that, they could also find them both interesting and challenging to take on. You should probably question why these tasks seem to form part of your responsibilities at all and why you have not already delegated them.

- Tasks you **can** delegate. These are jobs which others could be doing if they were fully capable of doing so. Delegating these tasks provides them with the opportunity to develop their skills, so long as you ensure that the necessary coaching or training is forthcoming to enable them to acquire the requisite skills.

- Tasks you must **retain**. These are the jobs which are your core responsibilities, such as planning ahead for future action; selecting someone new; monitoring people's performance and effort; supporting, evaluating and rewarding people. If all or any of these activities impinge directly on your business, they are best carried out by you, unless you have a very able deputy.

This analysis is useful because it prompts you to realize that you may still be carrying out some tasks which you really should have delegated years ago. However, it does not mean that you should delegate the dreary tasks while keeping all the attractive ones yourself. Nor can you delegate work which you find difficult. If you have problems, it is unlikely that other people will do any better than you.

Knowing What the Task Requires

Once you have decided to delegate a specific task, the next step is to make certain you know precisely what it involves. Something which you do without much thought because you have done it for ages might look, on the surface, to be a fairly routine task. But it may turn out to require a personal touch that only you can provide, or an in-depth skill that no-one else has (which is often why you are doing what you're doing in the first place). This means analyzing what the task requires and identifying:

- The **mental processes** needed to carry out the task.

- The **activities** to be performed and the equipment to be used in the task.

- The **relationships** with other people necessary to complete the task.

So consider the skills and abilities necessary to carry out the work. For example:

Overhauling the filing system. You are unable to find things quickly so you need to sort out how things are stored. This involves:

- **Mental processes:** logical thinking.
- **Activities:** sorting files; putting things in order.
- **Relationships:** consulting with others.

Customising a standard letter. You have an annual mailing to your customers and need a standard letter which has to be made to appear individual. This involves:

- **Mental processes:** decision-making.
- **Activities:** writing letters; using word processor.
- **Relationships:** understanding customer needs.

Organizing a Presentation. It has been decided to hold a presentation in order to make people more aware of the products and services the company offers. This involves:

- **Mental processes:** ability to plan.
- **Activities:** organizing and directing.
- **Relationships:** liaising with other people to get their co-operation.

By considering the attributes required for each task, you will get a more precise idea of what would give the job a better than average chance of being done well by someone else.

Assessing the Risks

Delegating requires you to pass on some of your responsibility and authority for carrying out tasks while still being accountable. It is important to appreciate that if something goes wrong once the task is delegated, it is the person doing the delegating who remains responsible. So before delegating any of the tasks you have selected as suitable, you need to evaluate how much of a risk you will be taking when you pass on a job for which you are ultimately answerable.

In practical terms, this means assessing:

- **How much risk?** What are consequences of the job being mismanaged, and what are the chances of that happening?

- **How much responsibility?** What obligations which you are relied upon to care about are you handing over?

- **How much authority?** What extent of your command and control will you be giving up?

This is not always as simple as it sounds; for instance it is possible to have the responsibility for, say, a budget, and yet not have the authority to spend it. A task you have selected for delegation may come well within the categories of '**must**', '**should**' and '**can**', yet not pass a risk assessment test. It is only by being aware of all that the task involves in terms of accountability that you can be sure you will not be taking unwarranted risks which could put your jurisdiction in jeopardy.

Summary: Analyzing the Job

Delegating requires you to take stock of your activities and sort those tasks which you can and should delegate from those which you need to retain.

By analyzing the nature of the job to be delegated and pin-pointing the necessary skills and abilities needed to carry out the task, you will determine what is required for the job to be done properly. By gauging the amount of risk, responsibility and authority the task incorporates, you can minimize the inherent dangers in delegating.

In this way you are able to make a wise choice about which jobs would be most suitable for delegating.

Questions to Ask Yourself

Think about your work and ask yourself the following questions:

♣ Are there tasks I am still doing which I **must** and **should** delegate?

♣ Are there tasks I **can** delegate, if only there was someone able to do them?

♣ Have I identified the tasks I cannot delegate and need to **retain**?

♣ Do I have an idea of the skills and abilities involved in a job before I delegate it?

♣ Do I know what responsibilities the job entails?

♣ Do I know what authority will have to be delegated?

♣ Have I assessed the risks?

♣ Do I understand that I will always remain accountable for the tasks I delegate?

You Will Be Doing Better If...

★ You know which tasks you **must, should** and **can** delegate.

★ You know which tasks you need to **retain**.

★ You analyze the skills and abilities required for the job before you delegate it.

★ You are aware of the responsibilities involved.

★ You know the extent of the authority you may hand over.

★ You have assessed the risks.

★ You accept that you will always be accountable for the tasks you delegate.

3.   Deciding Who Can Do It

Once you have decided which tasks can and should be done by others, you have to decide who could do them. Not everybody is at the same stage of development in their knowledge and skills; some may be extremely able and experienced, some may not have had an opportunity to use their skills; and others may have learned the rudiments and require coaching and encouragement.

So, the first thing you have to do is consider the level of ability that people possess.

Considering Capabilities

When deciding who might do a particular task, you should start by consulting your list of skills and then consider the capabilities of the people available.

You are likely to find that people tend to fall into three categories when you come to determine their abilities:

- **The Aces**. These are experienced people. It is essential that they are left alone once the task has been handed over, unless help is requested. If it is, you should take any such requests for help very seriously. The last thing you want is for an accomplished person to have to say, "I wouldn't have come to you for advice if I knew what I should be doing".

- **The Kings and Queens**. These are fairly experienced people, but need support from time to time. It is important to check progress intermittently and monitor unobtrusively while giving encouragement.

- **The Jacks**. These people need to learn how to do the task so you may not have considered them at all. But a lack of experience should not be confused with a lack of ability. They ought to be told how to carry out the task and given feedback if they are to gain confidence and learn quickly.

There is also another category, often forgotten, namely:

- **The Jokers**. These are the outsiders in the pack who can be called upon when the need arises. Their real value comes to the fore when an urgent task or a specialized job has to be completed, because they can provide specific skills. When you are overwhelmed by the amount you have to do remember that, no matter what the job, there is usually someone somewhere who can fill the breach.

Recognizing the various levels of ability which people possess means that you will only need to provide assistance for those who require it, and you can leave those who are well able to do the job to their own devices. If you do not get this right, you may leave the less experienced people to struggle on with something they cannot handle, while more experienced people see you as interfering unnecessarily in a task they can complete standing on their heads.

By tailoring the amount of assistance you provide to the capabilities of different people, you will improve those who need improving and encourage those who are already competent to remain so. This way, everyone can only get better. The object is to train your Jacks, motivate your Kings and Queens, and land up with all your cards being Aces.

Knowing What People Need

For people to be capable of carrying out the tasks delegated to them, they need to **know the facts** and **feel supported**.

To know exactly what is required of them, they should be made fully aware of:

● The area of responsibility being delegated, its ramifications and its boundaries, so that they are absolutely clear about the degree to which you are making them accountable.

- The amount of authority you are delegating which will enable them to carry out the task. This includes informing others who are directly involved about the authority you have delegated, so that the task can be done without encountering blockages.

- The standards which you require and the time-scale involved, so that they know precisely what is expected of them and within what period the task is to be carried out.

As well as understanding the extent and criteria of the delegated task, people need to feel they will be encouraged in their efforts. For this they need to know that:

- You will be fully supportive while the task is being carried out so that if they are unable to handle something, they can always come back to you and discuss it.

- You care about the task and want them to be successful in completing it.

- You have confidence in them and their abilities.

Too many people who delegate tasks concentrate on the factual areas and fail to realize that the psychological areas are of equal importance, if not more so.

Matching Tasks to People

Ideal delegation is that which assigns a task to a person who is competent to do it and who will find it stimulating and challenging.

To get as near as possible to this ideal you should look at the task you have decided to delegate and match it against the skills of the people who might best execute it. For example:

- A task you **must** delegate, such as overhauling the filing system. Since this involves classifying and arranging the files, it will require someone with an orderly mind. For a person who needs to learn more, it could be an interesting as well as informative task, so this is one that is suitable for a Jack.

- A task you **should** delegate, such as a standard letter you send out regularly but which requires customising to each recipient. Since this involves basic keyboard skills, common sense and an interest in others, it would provide extra scope for someone who is keen to take on more responsibility and could be eminently suitable for a King or Queen.

- A task you **can** delegate, such as the organization of a presentation. Since this involves planning, co-ordinating and dealing with people, you will need someone who is good at making decisions and taking responsibility. An Ace might enjoy such an opportunity.

Even if there does not appear to be an ideal person to carry out a particular task, there will usually be someone who is capable of tackling some part of it. By handing over that aspect, you can enable the person to get the feel of the whole task, and once relevant skills have been developed, the whole task can then be delegated.

Summary: Analyzing People

Choosing the right people to carry out certain tasks requires you to analyze not only their abilities, but also what might interest and challenge them.

It is a bit like providing the moist, hot atmosphere in a tropical plant conservatory. If you do not get the conditions right, the plants cannot flower.

As with growing rare orchids, delegating can only be effective when you understand what is needed to stimulate the best results.

Questions to Ask Yourself

Think about the people available to carry out specific tasks and answer the following questions:

♠ Do I know the level of knowledge and skills that each person possesses?

♠ Have I identified the sorts of tasks that would be most suitable for Aces or Kings and Queens?

♠ Do I know which tasks a Jack could easily learn to do?

♠ Am I clear about the facts people need to know in order to do the task?

♠ Do I understand the importance of psychological support?

♠ Do I try to matchmake between skills and tasks?

You Will Be Doing Better If...

★ You assess the capabilities of different people.

★ You are clear which tasks would be appropriate for Aces, Kings and Queens.

★ You know which tasks could be done by a Jack with a bit of help.

★ You have identified the facts people need to know in order to carry out the task.

★ You understand the importance of giving encouragement and support to those doing it.

★ You try to suit the right tasks to the right people.

4. Briefing

Once you have worked out which task (or tasks) you want to delegate and to whom, you need to brief the person who will be doing the job.

This requires you set the scene, talk over the details, define the standards and, having assigned the task, set up a system for reporting on progress.

Setting the Scene

The scene should be set by introducing the task you wish to delegate. You need to cover three basic points:

- **What you want doing**. For example: "I'd like you to take over the arrangements for our next presentation."

- **Why it needs to be done**. "We have found that by meeting our customers this way, we can show them our new products very effectively."

- **How it fits into the overall picture**. "The presentation forms a key element in our marketing strategy. It is important because it allows us to follow up and develop the specific interests expressed by different customers ."

Then you need to personalize the task and obtain commitment by giving your reasons for choosing the

31

individual, and indicating your confidence in his or her ability to do the work. "I've chosen you for this because you've often said you'd like to be given extra responsibility and I'm certain that you'll do a really good job."

After this, you need to elicit the person's reactions to the idea of the job. "How do you feel about taking this on?" In this way you will be able to assess his or her willingness to accept the task. This also provides an opportunity for the individual to voice any doubts, and for you to give reassurance. For instance, "You write good basic letters, and I think that if you and I work on a few of the more complex ones, you should easily be able to do them yourself."

Talking Over the Details

Once the scene is set, you can go on to discuss the task in some depth. This means talking over what the the job entails, what responsibility is involved, and what authority will be given. For example, when delegating the customised letter, you need to clarify:

- **The responsibilities you are handing over**. "I'd like you to take charge of writing the customised letters. You will be responsible for sending them out as well as filing them. You will need to check the list of all our customers and make sure it is up-to-date."

- **The components of the task**. "If you read the current standard letter and go through each of the 12 customer files you will familiarize yourself with their previous needs and be able to update their requirements. Then you can consider how the letter might be tailored to fit each customer's individual needs."

- **The authority you are assigning**. "You can introduce yourself as the person in charge of our public relations, so that people will know they are to deal directly with you."

Joint discussion about what needs to be done enables others to understand exactly what is required. It involves them in analyzing how the task can be completed and allows them to start working out how they will go about tackling it.

Describing the Background

As well as spelling out the details of the task, you need to give people the background to the work, so that they do not find themselves having to cope with aspects of the task for which they are totally unprepared. While you know the full picture, others do not, so the person concerned must be told the context in which the task is carried out – its possible pitfalls, the foibles of any personalities involved, etc. For the presentation, for instance, this would include:

- A potted history of previous presentations, what worked well, what went wrong: "By and large, the hotel we have used has looked after us very well, but the projector we hired was faulty so you might want to find another supplier this."

- The format that is usually followed and why: "We have a short presentation, followed by questions which enables people to air their concerns."

- The details about the venue: "The hall we usually use is... and the person you need to contact is.... Mr. Biggins is rather difficult but his assistant, Mr. Whapshot, is extremely competent and cannot do enough to help."

It is worth spelling out intimate, and usually unwritten, details because if the task is to be delegated properly, it is essential that people know what to expect as well as what to do.

Setting the Standards

The next step is to set the standards. People who are taking on tasks need criteria against which to measure their performance. they also have to know whether what they are doing is actually what is wanted. Defining the standards involves indicating the results required, not necessarily specifying the methods of achieving them. It is only required of you to tell people how to do the task when it is clear that they really do not know how.

You set standards by considering four basic elements: quantity, quality, time and cost. So, when reorganizing the filing system, the standards would look like this:

- The **quantity** required: all the files should be sorted and labelled.

- The **quality** needed: all the files should be labelled in a standard way and colour-coded according to type.

- The **time** constraints: the reorganization must be completed by the end of the month which is the end of the financial year.

- The **costs** involved: new materials required for the job should not cost more than it did last year.

Setting standards for the job allows the person who is taking on the task to be fully aware of what is expected and able to judge how he or she is doing against the benchmarks. More importantly, it gives you a yardstick by which to gauge his or her performance.

Coaching

As part of the briefing, you need to review existing skills and identify whether there are any areas where coaching is required in order to do the task.

While Jacks will almost certainly require coaching before you allow them to get on with the job independently, you can as easily encounter an Ace who needs help. An executive secretary, for instance, could find that 20 years' experience may count for very little when confronted with a brand new word processing package.

It is essential that coaching is a joint effort and this means working with those doing the task rather than dictating how you want things done. There are two important aspects of coaching: one is to **guide** people to use their own initiative and logic, and the other is to **instruct** them in a skill.

For many jobs the guiding element is usually sufficient to get someone under way, and may encompass all that is necessary by way of coaching. For this, you will need to:

- Ask logical questions to help them deduce how to do something for themselves.

- Provide information when they genuinely cannot work things out for themselves or, better still, let them know where they can find it.

- Encourage them to make their own decisions. (If this includes designing their own solutions, so much the better.)

For other jobs where there is a need to be taught some form of practical skill, instruction is the vital element of coaching. This is a process which should always be done by example. There are four stages:

1. Show how it is done in the normal way.
2. Repeat it slowly, explaining what you are doing.
3. Get the individual to do it while you talk him or her through the process; then
4. Get them to do it on their own.

Coaching enables people to take on the responsibility not only for carrying out the task in hand but also for continuing their own learning.

Reporting Progress

At the end of the briefing, you have to discuss and agree how you will monitor and support the person doing the task. You must be able to check that things are going according to plan and to do this in a way that is perceived to be helpful. The person doing the task needs to feel that there is a framework within which to report progress. "We can discuss how you are doing on a weekly basis, but if you have any qualms at all, please come and discuss things at once."

Determining a course of action for what has been agreed during the briefing enables people to feel properly organized and supported. This involves:

- Making a jointly-agreed plan of how the delegated task will be monitored. "We need to agree a time-scale for the job, and how we can ensure that things go according to plan."

- Arranging a follow-up meeting to take place during or after the event (or a series of meetings if the task is a long-term one). "Can we meet again next week to see how you are getting on?"

- Reminding the person that you are always there for consultation. "Remember that if you need anything, you need not hesitate to ask."

Once the task is assigned and the reporting system is in place, you have to let people get on with the task. You also need to appreciate that other people may well do things in different ways from you and their way may in fact be better than yours. By allowing others the freedom to do things their way, so long as the objectives and standards are met, you enable them to develop their skills, gain confidence and enjoy doing the work.

Summary: Handing Over the Task

Delegating always needs to be carried out in a systematic and structured way. It is a bit like building a house of cards. If the base is not firmly and solidly constructed, the edifice cannot stand up for very long. Briefing is the cornerstone which supports your house and enables you to delegate effectively.

When people are sure what is expected of them, are clear about what they need to achieve, and know why they have been assigned a specific task, they have the best possible prospects of doing well.

Questions to Ask Yourself

Think about how you brief people when delegating and answer the following questions:

♦ Do I set the scene in a way which lets people know what the job is about?

♦ Do I let people know I consider them the best person for the job?

♦ Do I jointly discuss the details of what is to be done?

♦ Do I give people the low-down on the job?

♦ Do I set the standards required?

♦ Do I establish whether coaching is needed?

♦ Do I guide and instruct where necessary?

♦ Do I set up an agreed reporting system?

You Will Be Doing Better If...

★ You set the scene to ensure that people understand what is required.

★ You impart your confidence in their ability to do the job.

★ You have a joint discussion to determine what the task requires.

★ You fill in the detailed background information to the job.

★ You define the standards you require.

★ You check whether someone needs coaching in some aspect of the task.

★ You encourage and instruct when needed.

★ You agree what needs to done and arrange follow-up meetings at appropriate intervals.

★ You brief well enough to hand over the task and let a person get on with it.

5.   Monitoring Progress

Delegating is not about leaving someone to get on with something you have no time to do yourself and forgetting about it. It is about getting the bulk of the task done by someone else and then checking the work. You need to make sure that the job is done, and done properly.

Part of the time in which you are left free to get on with other things should be devoted to monitoring the delegated task. This need not take more than a fraction of the time gained, but it is a vital part of delegating and, if you do not do it, you could end up with a great deal more work than you had before.

Checking

The real challenge facing you is to monitor progress without interfering in the work that someone else is doing. The one thing that is sure to kill anyone's enthusiasm for a task is if you keep popping up demanding "How're you getting on?"

With certain people or tasks you may only need to check the work on completion. With others you need to keep a weather-eye on what is going on so as to spot any dark clouds which might be gathering on the horizon. This means monitoring events at intervals by comparing:

- What should be happening.

- What is actually happening.

- Whether there is any substantial variation between the two.

If there is a marked difference between what should be happening and what is happening, effort on your part is obviously required. You will have to initiate prompt corrective action to get things back on track. But first you need to decide how serious the shortfall is, and what can be done to rectify the situation. Then you can take appropriate steps – in order of magnitude of the difficulty as you see it:

- **Minor**. When you think events may not be on schedule, arrange a meeting to discuss possible problems. By obtaining an up-to-date progress report you may find that the person concerned is well aware of, and in control of, the situation.

- **Major**. When it appears that things are way off course, offer support to resolve the difficulties. Make it clear that you are not apportioning blame and state that you will do anything you can to help.

- **Mega**. When it looks as if a disaster is impending, take over the task and see it to a reasonable conclusion, if this is still possible.

Those who are carrying out delegated tasks are probably aware that things have got out of hand, so it serves little purpose to remonstrate with them. More often than not, it is because they did not ask for help soon enough that they got out of their depth. So giving your support while sorting out the difficulty is a necessary part of delegating and allows the individual concerned to learn from the experience.

In most instances, once things have been resolved it is worthwhile letting people have another try. If you do not think so, perhaps you need to consider whether you had too high an opinion of their abilities and if perhaps they should tackle another less demanding or more low-risk task.

Advising

Sometimes people will ask you what you think they should do when carrying out a certain aspect of their task. Even though you know exactly what should be done, you should always ask "What do *you* think you should do?"

Most of the time they already have a sensible answer but just lack the confidence to put it into practice. By bouncing the question back to them, you prevent them from becoming over-dependent on you and encourage them to treat the task as their own.

Reviewing

When a job is completed, it is often a good idea to review the task with the person who carried it out, especially if he or she is a novice. When reviewing a person's work you need to:

- Compare the results with the standards that were set earlier and discuss how the task was performed.

- Congratulate the person on things that went well.

- Ask the individual what he or she has learned from taking on the work and help to identify any areas where improvement is needed.

By giving people the opportunity to look back at how they discharged the task, you enable them to consolidate their learning and to recognize their own achievements.

Giving Credit

Once people have successfully carried out their delegated tasks, their success should be fully recognized. As the essence of delegating is to pass on the responsibility and authority for a task while you still remain accountable for the results, the temptation to take the credit for getting a job done can sometimes prove too much. But if you are to ensure that people continue to accept delegated tasks and enjoy carrying them out, public and whole-hearted acknowledgement of their efforts and their successes is essential.

Since you are delegating the task in the first place, there is no need to prove (either to yourself or to others) that you can do it better than most. Crediting someone else for a job well done may make all the difference to their lives and not a jot of difference to yours.

Summary: Keeping Track

Even when people are on top of a task, they will still need checking and encouragement. They cannot simply be cast adrift on the ocean waves to weather the storms and the sharks.

You need to follow their progress without it appearing as if you are watching their every move and they need to feel that they are being allowed to get on with the job and make their own decisions.

At the end of the job, you ought to review the work to help people weigh up what they have achieved. Most of all, you should give people full credit for their efforts when the task is successfully completed.

Questions to Ask Yourself

Think about how you monitor progress and answer the following questions:

♦ Do I keep track of progress without interfering?

♦ Do I do a spot check on what should be happening and compare it with what is?

♦ Do I take remedial action if there are problems?

♦ Do I encourage people to come up with their own answers to problems?

♦ Do I review what has been achieved with the person concerned?

♦ Do I congratulate people for a job well done?

♦ Do I give people full credit for their work?

You Will Be Doing Better If...

★ You monitor progress without interfering.

★ You occasionally check and make comparisons between what should be happening and what is happening.

★ You sort out problems promptly.

★ You help people to overcome any difficulties they experience.

★ You encourage people to find their own solutions.

★ You review how the task was performed.

★ You congratulate people for their good work.

★ You give credit unreservedly when and where it is due.

6.   Attitudes to Delegating

Delegating is a two-way process. If you are prepared to let go, trust people and support their mistakes, they will commit themselves and give their best in return.

It is only by having the right attitude that you are likely to generate the right attitude in others.

Letting Go

Letting go is often easier said than done. It is about having the courage to take a calculated risk by deciding to let someone else to do a task that you would normally do, while still accepting full responsibility for the results. People have difficulty in letting go because they are afraid that others will do something awful that they would never have done themselves. They also dread losing control.

You need to remind yourself that:

- You are not the only person who is capable of doing the things you do.

- As long as the job is done to the required standard, it does not matter if it is not done the way you would do it.

- You will not lose control of your work overall, if you let go of a part of it.

You should have faith in the fact that if you choose wisely and delegate well enough, you will get good results.

Showing Trust

Showing that you trust people to do the task properly will go a long way to ensure that it is.

Trust is built up gradually and can be initiated by asking people to carry out less important tasks before you delegate anything of greater importance to them. For example, you probably would not delegate the organization of the presentation to a Jack, but you might do so once he or she had successfully reorganized the filing system.

It is up to you to build trust by:

- Always doing what you have promised you will do. So, if you say you will provide a certain piece of equipment, then be sure to do so.

- Regularly indicating that you value the effort others have made towards achieving results. This can be as simple as saying thank you, sincerely and directly.

- Never letting those who are doing a delegated task take the blame for anything that goes wrong. This means defending them publicly and remedying it privately.

If problems occur, people need to be certain that you will stand up for them and be loyal to them. If you do not, they will learn not to trust you and will not give the job their best efforts because they think that you will probably let them down at the first sign of trouble.

People need to feel sure that they will never be abandoned when carrying out the job they have been trusted to do. This way, not only do they feel that you trust them, but they will trust you.

Supporting Mistakes

People must be 'allowed' to make mistakes. You do not want people to make mistakes if they can help it, but inevitably mistakes will happen. The important thing is to let it be known that if something goes wrong people should not be afraid to admit it. "If anything horrible happens, please don't hug it to yourself; tell me instantly and we'll get it sorted." This gives them the confidence that you will support them and that your attitude will always be constructive and helpful, no matter what the circumstances.

If you have not conveyed your willingness to support mistakes, people will not bring you their problems. They will be afraid of a hostile reaction and will try to hide what has happened. So when you finally find out, you will almost certainly have to sort out a crisis, which should never have got to that pitch in the first place. This not only affects your own work, but will also cause the person doing the task to lose heart.

If people are confident that you have their interests at heart, it is reciprocated. They work hard to ensure that they will not let you down.

Obtaining Commitment

Since you will be handing over a certain amount of authority and responsibility, you need to feel that this will be properly used. Whatever the size of the task, anything that is delegated will always be the better for a degree of commitment. In fact, the more commitment you can obtain from those to whom you delegate, the greater the chance that they will be successful.

To take on the task and its attendant responsibilities, people need to be interested, willing and able. Ability without a willingness to take on a task generally means that it will not be satisfactorily completed. One volunteer is worth a hundred pressed men, so taking time to ensure that people are committed to carrying out the job is worth any effort involved.

To obtain commitment, you need to convince people that:

- They are carrying out a task which is necessary. (This makes it seem worthwhile and makes people feel that, however small, it plays a significant part in a larger whole.)

- They have a certain degree of autonomy within which to operate, provided the objectives are met. (This allows people to prove themselves while having the satisfaction of doing it their own way.)

- They have been entrusted with the task because they are considered capable of doing it. (This will stretch their abilities and increase their self-esteem and self-confidence.)

In this way, you help people to become committed to the job, and encourage them to treat the task as their own, something to be proud of and not just something that they are doing to relieve someone else. Commitment breeds conscientiousness and it is this that carries people through the awkward or less pleasant parts of the task in order to achieve ultimate success.

If you do not confirm an individual's willingness and interest to take over the task, you have no guarantee that it will be done properly or even carried out at all – which entirely defeats the purpose of delegating it in the first place.

Summary: Delegating Successfully

Knowing how to delegate may be your main aim, but without the right attitude, all your efforts may well come to nothing.

Feeling reluctant to delegate will hold you back from enjoying the many advantages of doing so. If you allow yourself to let go some of your work you will unburden yourself and release your energies for other things.

You need to believe in people and trust them to do a good job. You also need to give them your unstinting support. If you behave in this way, people will feel that their skills are appreciated and that what they are doing is important.

But none of this can happen unless you adopt the attitude that everyone has the capacity to do as good a job as you can.

Questions to Ask Yourself

Think about your attitude to delegating and answer the following questions:

♥ Do I make a real effort to let go?

♥ Am I prepared to trust people?

♥ Do I always do what I promise to do?

♥ Do I stand up for people when trouble occurs?

♥ Do I support people whole-heartedly?

♥ Do I convince people that the task they are doing is worthwhile?

♥ Do I encourage people to treat the task as their own?

♥ Do I feel I get people's commitment?

♥ Do I consider that I have the right attitude to delegating?

You Will Be Doing Better If...

★ You are prepared to let go of various tasks and allow others to prove their abilities.

★ You are able to trust people.

★ You keep your promises.

★ You support people at all times.

★ You take the blame if there are any problems.

★ You back up people when they need it.

★ You obtain people's commitment to carry out the task.

★ You are aware that the right attitude is an essential constituent of successful delegating.

Check List for Delegating

If you are finding that delegating is proving to be more difficult than you expected, and your attempts to delegate are not meeting with success, think about whether this is because you have failed to take account of one or more of the following aspects:

Choosing the Task

If a job has not been done to your satisfaction, perhaps it is because you have not fully understood the importance of identifying which tasks you can and cannot delegate. Perhaps you chose a task that had too much responsibility or you did not delegate the authority necessary to do the job properly. Possibly you did not assess the risks involved before delegating it. Or it could be that you did not take account of precisely what was involved in carrying out the task.

Choosing the People

If the evidence proves that you have chosen the wrong person for the job, maybe it is because you did not correctly assess the individual's capabilities, or you failed to match the task to his or her interests and abilities. Perhaps you did not realize the degree of personal support that was required, or you never obtained full commitment.

Briefing

If you find that people are struggling to do what you have asked them, it may be that they do not fully understand the nature of the job because you did not brief them properly. You may not have given them sufficient information, or you may not have filled them in on the background details so they are not properly equipped to cope. You may even have neglected to set the standards for the job or failed to check that they were sure of what they had to do before starting.

Monitoring Progress

If nothing seems to be going right, it may be that you have not kept an eye on what was happening and whether people were doing what they should be doing. Perhaps you did not arrange to obtain feedback and so could not correct things before they got out of hand.

Your Attitude to Delegating

If people seem to lack interest in the job, perhaps you gave them the impression that you could do the job better than they could, or that you were reluctant to give it to them in the first place. Having assigned the task, you need to have the courage of your convictions and believe that others are just as capable of doing a good job as you are.

The Benefits of Delegating

Delegating gives you an opportunity to achieve so much more than just getting other people to carry out various tasks. It offers you a chance to improve productivity and helps you to manage yourself more effectively at one and the same time.

The main benefits to be gained from delegating are:

- You get more done, including many of the things you always wanted to do.

- You get to know people better and so enhance relationships.

- You help other people to develop and to increase their self-confidence.

- You gain time to devote to strategic activities like thinking and planning.

- You learn to let go.

The more you delegate properly, the easier managing becomes. Once you have taken the step towards assigning a task in an organized way, you will readily find the courage to let people get on with it. And once you have experienced the benefits which can be gained from delegating, then the rewards are yours for the taking.

Glossary

Here are some definitions in relation to Delegating.

Accountability – Having to suffer the consequences if something goes wrong with the job.

Authority – Having the power to influence or command people, in the full expectation that they will do what they are asked to do.

Briefing – Giving enough information to someone else to enable him or her to be a surrogate you.

Coaching – Demonstrating by deed or by implication to bring about an immediate result.

Credit – Commendation for a job well done.

Delegating – Assigning work to someone else while still having to carry the can.

Encouraging – Inspiring someone to have the confidence to do something.

Letting go – Relinquishing without reluctance.

Mistakes – Blunders big and small.

Monitoring – Keeping track of progress while seeming not to do so.

Praising – Expressing complete and unreserved approval or admiration.

Reporting back – Giving a good account of all that has happened so far. You hope.

Responsibility – Having obligations and duties in relation to the job and beyond it.

Risk – The gamble you take when delegating, greatly reduced by doing it properly.

Skill – The knowledge or experience derived from direct participation.

Supporting – Being a source of strength by defending, fostering, and propping up.

Task – An assigned piece of work.

Trusting – Placing sufficient confidence in others that they accomplish tasks without fear or misgivings.

The Author

Kate Keenan is a Chartered Occupational Psychologist with degrees in affiliated subjects (B.Sc., M.Phil.) and a number of qualifications in others.

She founded Keenan Research, an industrial psychology consultancy, in 1978. The work of the consultancy is fundamentally concerned with helping people to achieve their potential and make a better job of their management.

By devising work programmes for companies she enables them to target and remedy their managerial problems – from personnel selection and individual assessment to team building and attitude surveys. She believes in giving priority to training the managers to institute their own programmes, so that their company resources are developed and expanded.

Having always believed in the maxim that if you want a good job doing you should do it yourself, Kate Keenan has finally realized that delegating is a powerful method by which others can be helped to do as good a job as she does (if not better). This relieves her of the necessity to do it all, at the same time as enabling her to do a great deal more than ever before.

THE MANAGEMENT GUIDES

Available now:

	Book £2.99	Tape £4.99
Communicating	☐	
Delegating	☐	
Making Time*	☐	☐
Managing*	☐	☐
Managing Yourself*	☐	☐
Motivating*	☐	☐
Negotiating	☐	
Planning*	☐	☐
Running Meetings	☐	
Selecting People*	☐	☐
Solving Problems	☐	
Understanding Behaviour	☐	

These books are available at your local bookshop or newsagent, or can be ordered direct. Prices and availability are subject to change without notice. Just tick the titles you require and send a cheque or postal order for the value of the book to:

B.B.C.S., P.O. Box 941, HULL HU1 3VQ (24 hour Telephone Credit Card Line: 01482 224626), and add for postage & packing:

UK (& BFPO) Orders: £1.00 for the first book & 50p for each extra book up to a maximum of £2.50. Overseas (& Eire) Orders: £2.00 for the first book, £1.00 for the second & 50p for each additional book.

*These books are also available on audio tape by sending a cheque or postal order for the value of the tape to: Sound FX, The Granary, Shillinglee Park, Chiddingfold, Surrey GU8 4TA (Telephone: 01428 654623; Fax: 01428 707262), and add for postage & packing the same amount as specified for book postage above.